ALFRED'S BASIC ADULT
FINGER AEROBICS

Exercises to Develop the Strength, Flexibility and Agility of Each Finger

WILLARD A. PALMER • MORTON MANUS • AMANDA VICK LETHCO

FOREWORD

Most adults beginning to learn to play the piano find that they feel awkward at the keyboard because of stiffness in their fingers, hands and wrists. They have trouble with coordination, and they feel they could play much better if the muscular agility and flexibility of their hands could somehow be made to keep pace with their comprehension. FINGER AEROBICS is carefully planned and developed to help make this possible.

The word *aerobic* is generally applied to those exercises designed to condition the heart and lungs by increasing the intake of oxygen into the body. But the reason this oxygen intake is important to our well-being is that this oxygen is carried in the blood-stream to all parts of the body. If circulation of the arms, hands and fingers is not what it should be, this affects the ability for those parts of our body to function with precision and agility.

Many exercises are designed to fill the lungs with air, and to increase the strength of the larger muscles of the body, but few exercises focus on bringing agility to the fingers, hands and wrists. Most of our daily activities serve only to stiffen the fingers and dull their feelings and sensitivity. This includes using cooking utensils, screwdrivers, hammers, scissors and other small tools, as well as pushing lawn-mowers and grocery carts, lifting and moving large objects, etc. Adult hands take a beating, and little is done to care for them beyond an occasional application of skin lotion or a manicure. The exercises in this book are designed to increase the flow of oxygen to the fingers, and to help develop the strength, flexibility and agility of each individual finger muscle. They will also help you to play with relaxed fingers, wrists and arms.

FINGER AEROBICS is coordinated page-by-page with ALFRED'S BASIC ADULT PIANO COURSE, Lesson Book 1. The student may begin immediately with the Preliminary Exercises on pages 2 through 5, as well as the "TABLE-TOP AEROBICS" on page 48, and proceed after reaching page 12 in the Lesson Book. Instructions showing when to begin each new exercise appear at the upper right corner of each page.

Using these exercises daily will insure more rapid progress through all of the books of this course. Because fingers that are "warmed up" are more responsive, playing is made easier. You will be less likely to play wrong notes, and you will find that all technical challenges will be more easily met and enjoyed.

NATURAL BREATHING

Some people actually hold their breath when they are playing the piano, particularly if they are having difficulty with some particular problem. Needless to say, this inhibits circulation of oxygen to the hands as well as to the brain. Coordination becomes more difficult, and the fingers perform less efficiently.

One does not draw the stomach muscles IN to inhale naturally when seated at the piano. During inhalation, the lower abdomen moves OUTWARD a bit. When you exhale, it comes back in. Watch a baby breathing to get the idea.

It is important to breath easily and naturally as you play.

© Copyright MCMLXXXVIII by Alfred Publishing Co., Inc.

All rights reserved.   Printed in USA.

Preliminary Exercises

BE KIND TO YOUR HANDS!

No part of the body takes more abuse than the hands. We wear shoes on our feet to protect them against the rough surfaces they walk on. Our hands are almost constantly exposed to the elements and to the rough things we do to them. Gloves are usually worn only to keep the hands warm in cold weather.

If you want to keep your hands in playing condition, it is best to wear gloves when you are lifting large, heavy objects, as well as when you are working with rough tools, screwdrivers, pliers, wrenches, pruning shears, spades, and even vacuum cleaners.

USE A LITTLE WARM WATER

Before practicing, it is good to soak the hands for a few minutes in warm water. This promotes circulation. Many concert pianists use very warm water on their hands before beginning to play. Towel the hands vigorously until they are dry, then hold your arms out with the hands dangling from the wrist, and shake out your hands rapidly for a few moments.

DANGLE FROM
WRISTS

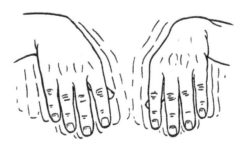

SHAKE OUT
HANDS

No. 1   **a)** Holding your arms in playing position, palms downward, clench both hands tightly, making two fists. Hold while you count "ONE-TWO."

MAKE TIGHT
FISTS

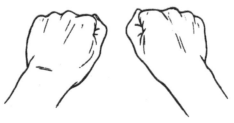

PALMS
DOWN

b) SNAP the fingers quickly outward, opening both hands. Do this with great vigor. Hold this position with all fingers extended. Count "THREE-FOUR."

SNAP
FINGERS OPEN

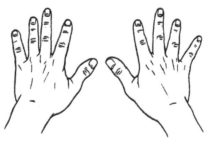

PALMS
DOWN

c) Shake out both hands, dangling from the wrists. Count "ONE-TWO-THREE-FOUR."

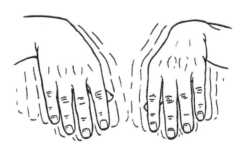

No. 2 **a)** Repeat the beginning of the previous exercise, with PALMS UPWARD. Clench both hands, making two fists. Hold and count "ONE-TWO."

MAKE TIGHT
FISTS

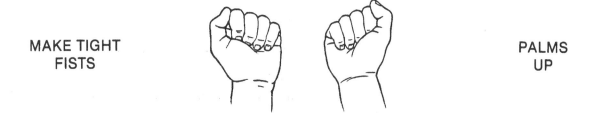

PALMS
UP

b) SNAP the fingers outward (palms up), opening both hands. Hold fingers outward as you count "THREE-FOUR."

SNAP
FINGERS OPEN

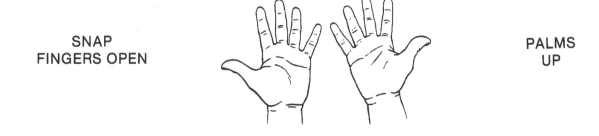

PALMS
UP

c) Turn hands over, palms down, hands dangling from the wrists, and shake out. Count "ONE-TWO-THREE-FOUR."

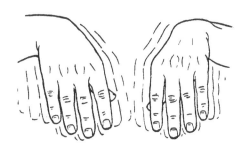

No. 3 **Combining DEEP-BREATHING with Preliminary Exercise No. 1**

Seated at the piano, repeat step **a)** of Preliminary Exercise No. 1, clenching the fists with palms downward, while breathing IN (the lower abdomen moves outward). Mentally count "ONE-TWO."

Repeat step **b)**, snapping the fingers outward, expelling the air while mentally counting "THREE-FOUR."

Repeat step **c)**, shaking out your hands as you inhale, mentally counting "ONE-TWO-THREE-FOUR." Continue as you exhale, counting "ONE-TWO-THREE-FOUR."

To avoid possible dizziness due to hyperventilation, this exercise should not be repeated more than two or three times at first.

No. 4 **Combining DEEP-BREATHING with Preliminary Exercise No. 2**

Follow the procedure described just above, clenching the hands and snapping the fingers outward with PALMS UP. Turn hands over to shake out from the wrists.

Isometric Exercise

An isometric exercise is one in which one set of muscles is briefly tensed in opposition to another set of muscles, or in opposition to a solid surface.

To prepare for this exercise, press the hands flatly together with all fingers touching, in a "prayer position."

Now slowly bring the palms apart, with fingertips touching, until all fingers are in a curved position.

EXERCISE: Keep fingers in the curved position, relaxed.

Now press the 3rd fingers firmly together. Keep the other fingers relaxed. Do this four times, COUNTING "ONE-TWO-THREE-FOUR."

Do the same with the 2nd fingers, then the 4th fingers, then the thumbs, and finally with the 5th fingers.

Repeat several times, then shake out your hands vigorously. Repeat again.

A Beneficial Hand Massage

1. Place the back of the left hand in the palm of the right hand, relaxed and flat.

2. With the thumb of the right hand, massage the left hand along the ridge of the fingers and along the fleshy part of the base of the thumb. Do not use excessive pressure, or you may bruise the hand. Continue this for about 30 seconds.

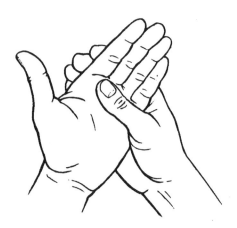

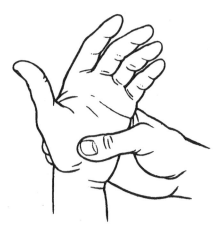

3. Reverse hands, massaging the right hand with the left.

4. Shake out the hands vigorously for several seconds.

This exercise should be beneficial to circulation and should make the hands more flexible.

Four Good Reasons for Playing with Curved Fingers

1. When the fingers are straight, each finger has a different length.

When the fingers are curved, each finger has, in effect, the same length.

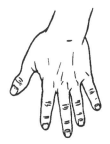 

2. If your fingers are straight, the thumb cannot be properly used.

Curved fingers bring the thumb into the correct playing position.

 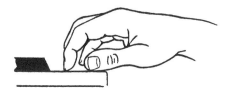

3. Straight fingers will bend at the first joint, opposite to the motion of the key, delaying key response.

With curved fingers, keys respond instantly. You are IN CONTROL when you CURVE!

 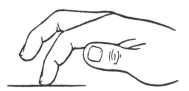

4. Moving over the keys will require turning the thumb *under* the fingers and crossing fingers *over* the thumb. Curved fingers provide an "ARCH" that makes this motion possible.

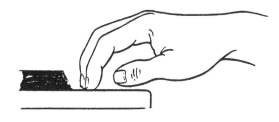

VERY IMPORTANT! Keep fingernails reasonably SHORT. It is impossible to curve fingers properly with long fingernails.

6

Five-Finger "Aerobics"

Use with pages 12 & 13 of Adult Lesson Book 1.

These workouts are played in CONTRARY MOTION. That is, the notes of the RH move UP as the notes of the LH move DOWN, and vice-versa. The hands play identical fingering at all times.

Play the first 8 measures of each of these workouts three times:

1. Moderately loud, keeping fingers close to the keys.
2. A little louder, lifting each finger about one inch above each key before you play it.
3. Much louder, lifting each finger as high as possible before playing.
   End the third time with the whole note in the last measure.

Play SLOWLY, with HANDS TOGETHER. Keep fingers CURVED at all times!

IMPORTANT! It is relaxing and helpful to take several deep breaths, exhaling slowly, before beginning any exercise. Breathe naturally as you play.

No. 1

No. 2

This exercise is a challenge for the weaker fingers (4–5).
These fingers will be strengthened with a little extra practice.

No. 3

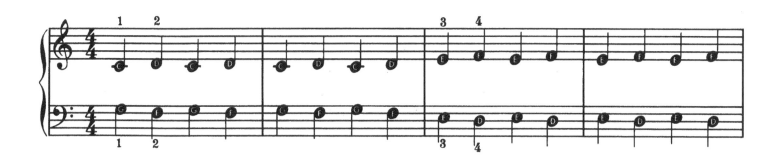

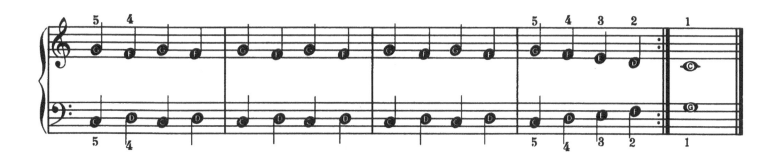

No. 4

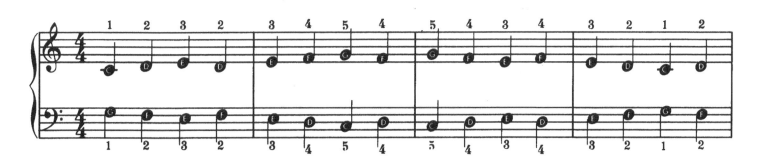

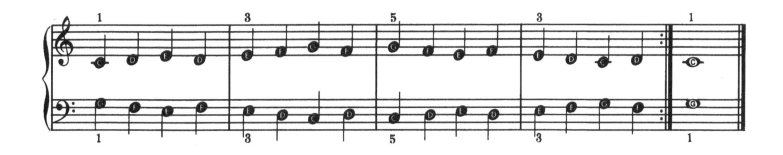

Wrist-Lifts (DANGLE & DROP, LOWER & LIFT)

Use with page 14.

1. DANGLE the right hand over E above middle C with the forearm HIGH. Let the hand hang limply from the wrist, with the tip of the 3rd finger a few inches above the key.

2. DROP the tip of 3 into the key.

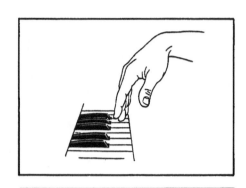

DANGLE and DROP

3. LOWER the forearm until the wrist is just about level with the tip of the 3rd finger. Do this in one continuous motion as you drop into the key on the count of "ONE."

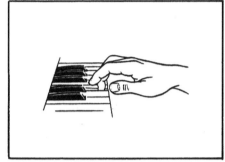

LOWER the forearm

4. LIFT the finger off the key by raising the forearm. The wrist will follow, then the fingers. Do this with a relaxed motion, on the count of "TWO."

   You are now back in starting position to repeat the exercise.

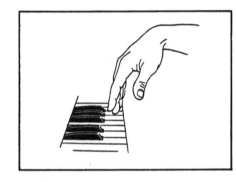

LIFT the forearm

These exercises will make your wrists more relaxed and flexible, and will help you produce more beautiful tones.

No. 1

DROP on "ONE," LIFT on "TWO," DROP on "THREE," LIFT on "FOUR," etc.

No. 2

Same exercise, using LEFT HAND on E below Middle C.

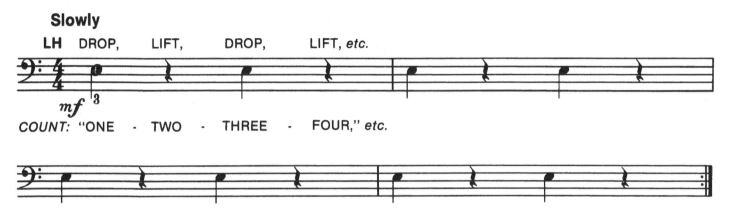

No. 3

Now try dropping the RH 3rd finger into different keys!

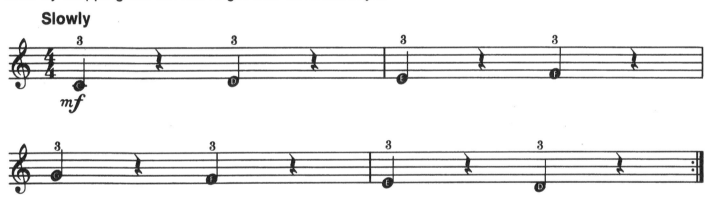

No. 4

Now drop LH 3 into different keys.

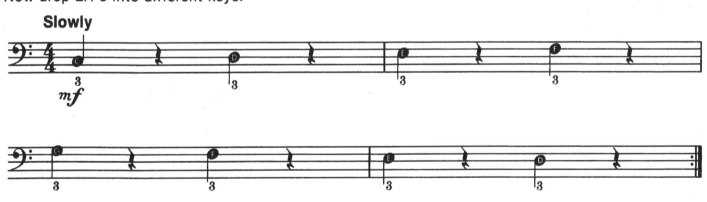

ADDING DEEP-BREATHING

Repeat Nos. 1–4 as follows:

    a) Take a deep breath as you dangle the hand from the wrist.

    b) Exhale slowly, expelling all the air from your lungs, as you DROP into the key.

    c) Inhale slowly and deeply as you LIFT the finger off the key.

    d) Continue the exercise, repeating steps b) & c).

Drops & Lifts On Melodic 2nds & 3rds

Use with page 14.

Breathe normally as you play these exercises.

No. 1 Melodic 2nds

In this exercise the hand position changes in each measure.

Connect each pair of notes smoothly together, dropping 2 on the first note and lifting 3 off the second note in one relaxed, continuous motion.

Notice that the RH begins with 2 & 3 on C & D and moves up to 2 & 3 on D & E, etc.

Moderately slow

COUNT: "DROP - LIFT - 3 - 4," etc.

(Continue up the keyboard as far as you wish.)

The LH begins with 2 & 3 on G & F and moves down to 2 & 3 on F & E, etc.

(Continue down the keyboard as far as you wish.)

No. 2 Melodic 3rds

The hand position changes in each measure.

Connect each pair of notes smoothly together, dropping 2 on the first note and lifting 4 off the second note in one relaxed, continuous motion.

The RH begins with 2 & 4 on C & E and moves up to 2 & 4 on E & F, etc.

Moderately slow

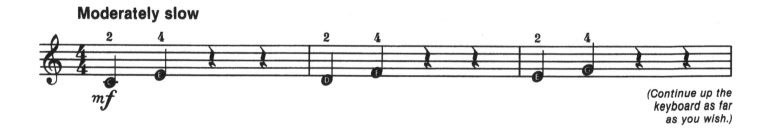

(Continue up the keyboard as far as you wish.)

The LH begins with 2 & 4 on G & E and moves down to 2 & 4 on F & D, etc.

(Continue down the keyboard as far as you wish.)

Use with page 15.

Drops & Lifts On Harmonic 2nds & 3rds

No. 1   Harmonic 2nds

The hand position changes in each measure.
Drop RH 2 & 3 on C & D. Lift off. In the next measure move 2 & 3 up to D & E, etc.

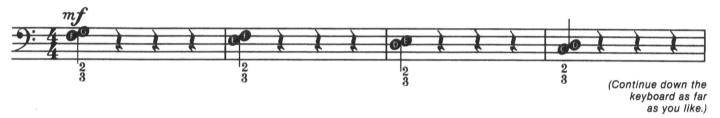

COUNT: "DROP-LIFT - 3 - 4," *etc.*

(Continue up the keyboard as far as you like.)

Drop LH 3 & 2 on LH F & G. In the next measure move 3 down to E & F, etc.

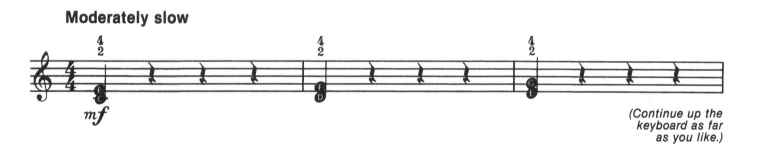

(Continue down the keyboard as far as you like.)

No. 2   Harmonic 3rds

The hand position changes in each measure.
Drop RH 2 & 4 on C & E. Lift off. In the next measure move 2 & 4 up to D & F, etc.

(Continue up the keyboard as far as you like.)

Drop LH 4 & 2 on E & G. In the next measure move 4 & 2 down to D & F, etc.

(Continue down the keyboard as far as you like.)

Dropping the Thumb

Use with page 16.

Because of the shape and the angle of the thumb with relation to the other fingers,
it must drop on its SIDE-TIP.

 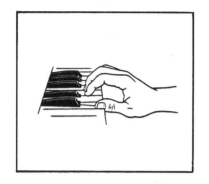 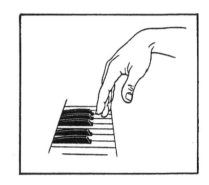

1. DANGLE *with thumb leading.*
2. DROP *on the SIDE-TIP.*

3. LOWER *the forearm.*

4. LIFT *the forearm.*

No. 1 2nds Up and Down the Keyboard, Dropping the Thumb

The hand position changes in each measure.

Connect each pair of notes smoothly together, dropping 1 on the first key and lifting 2 off the
second key in one relaxed, continuous motion.

The RH begins with 1 & 2 on C & D and moves up to 1 & 2 on D & E, etc.

Slow to Moderately slow

COUNT: "DROP-LIFT - 3 - 4," *etc.*

(Continue up the keyboard as far as you like.)

The LH begins with 1 & 2 on G & F and moves down to 1 & 2 on F & E, etc.

(Continue down the keyboard as far as you like.)

No. 2 Melodic 2nds, 3rds, 4ths & 5ths, Dropping the Thumb

This exercise is in C POSITION throughout.

Slow to Moderately slow

Use with page 17.

No. 3 Harmonic Intervals

This exercise is in C POSITION throughout.

Slow to Moderately slow

COUNT: "DROP - LIFT - 3 - 4," *etc.*

No. 4 Five-Finger Workout with 2nds & 3rds, Hands Together

This workout is played in PARALLEL MOTION. That is, the notes of the RH and LH move UP or DOWN together.

Play three times:

1. Soft, keeping fingers close to the keys.
2. Moderately loud, lifting each finger about one inch above the key.
3. Loud, lifting each finger high.

Moderately slow to Moderately fast

* *p-mf-f* means play *soft* the first time, *moderately loud* the second time, and *loud* the third time.

Drops & Lifts On C Major Chords

Use with pages 18 & 19.

IMPORTANT: Shape your hands (in the air) to play the correct keys before you begin each exercise.
The fingers and wrists should be relaxed, not stiff.

LH (MIRROR IMAGES) **RH**

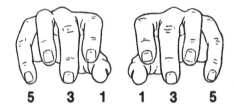

No. 1   Alternating Hands

Lift hands high (8 to 12 inches above the keyboard).
You may hold the damper pedal down throughout this exercise, if you wish.

Slow to Moderately slow

COUNT: "DROP-TWO-LIFT-FOUR, DROP-TWO-LIFT-FOUR," *etc.*

No. 2   Alternating Hands, Changing Octaves

Lift hands high.
You may hold the damper pedal down, if you wish.

Slow to Moderately slow

Both hands one octave (8 notes) higher . . . .

Both hands two octaves higher . . . . . .

Both hands one octave higher . . . . . .

No. 3 Hands Together, Changing Octaves

To make sure the wrists are relaxed, move the hands loosely up and down,
as if waving "good-bye," before you play.

DROP into each chord with pre-shaped, but relaxed fingers.

Lift the hands high for each rest, and move to the new octave position.

You may hold the damper pedal down, if you wish.

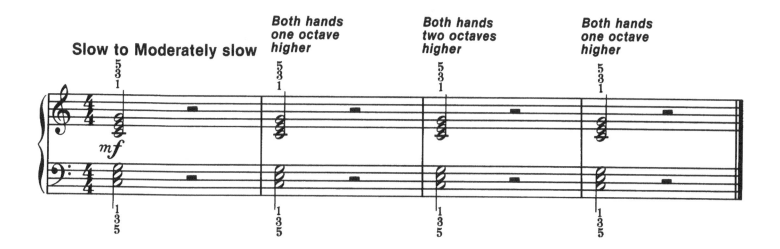

No. 4 Alternating Hands & Hands Together, Changing Octaves

Play three times:
1. Soft, keeping fingers close to the keys.
2. Moderately loud, lifting each finger about one inch above the key.
3. Loud, lifting each finger high.

You may hold the damper pedal down if you wish.

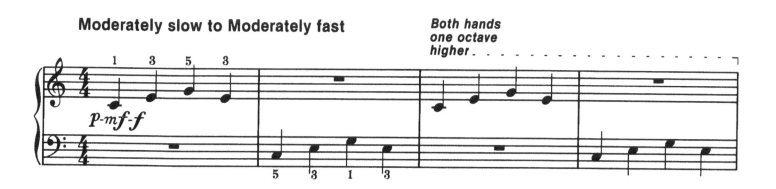

Use with pages 22 & 23.

Drops & Lifts on G⁷ Chords

IMPORTANT! Shape your hands (in the air) to play the correct keys before you begin each exercise. Always keep fingers and wrists relaxed.

LH (MIRROR IMAGES) **RH**

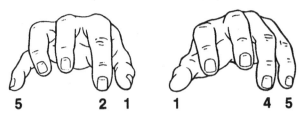

No. 1 Alternating Hands

Lift hands High.
You may hold the damper pedal down, if you wish.

Slow to Moderately slow

mf

COUNT: "DROP-TWO-LIFT-FOUR, DROP-TWO-LIFT-FOUR," *etc.*

No. 2 Alternating Hands, Changing Octaves

Lift hands high.
You may hold the damper pedal down, if you wish.

Slow to Moderately slow

Both hands one octave higher

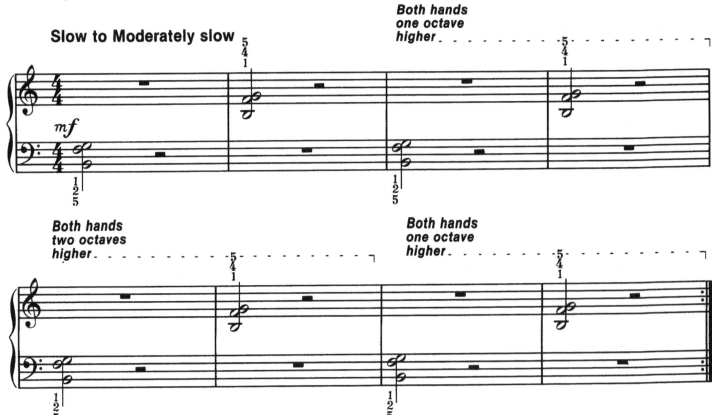

mf

Both hands two octaves higher

Both hands one octave higher

No. 3   Hands Together, Changing Octaves

Lift hands high.
You may hold the damper pedal down, if you wish.

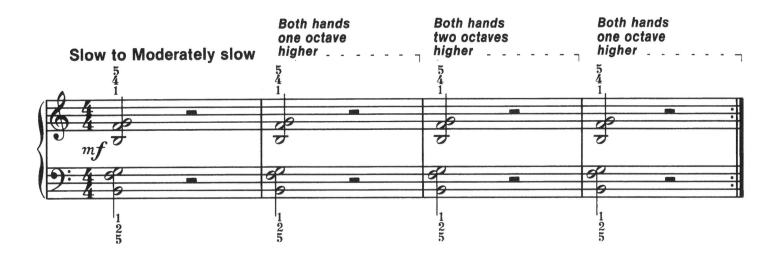

No. 4   Five-Finger Workout, Using the Notes of the C & G⁷ Chords

Play three times:
1. Soft, keeping fingers close to keys.
2. Moderately loud, lifting each finger about one inch above the key.
3. Loud, lifting each finger high.

Do NOT hold the damper pedal down in this exercise!

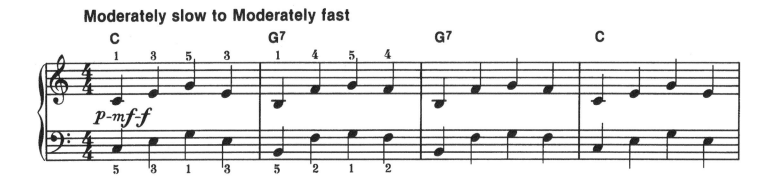

Drops & Lifts on F Major Chords

Use with pages 28 & 29.

IMPORTANT! Shape your hands (in the air) to play the correct keys before you begin each exercise. Always keep fingers and wrists relaxed.

LH (MIRROR IMAGES) **RH**

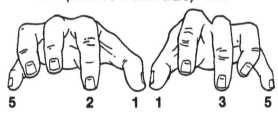

No. 1   Alternating Hands

Lift hands high.
You may hold the damper pedal down, if you wish.

Slow to Moderately slow

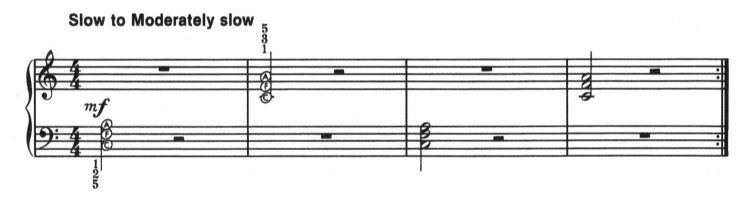

No. 2   Alternating Hands, Changing Octaves

Lift hands high.
You may hold the damper pedal down, if you wish.

Slow to Moderately slow

Both hands one octave higher

Both hands two octaves higher

Both hands one octave higher

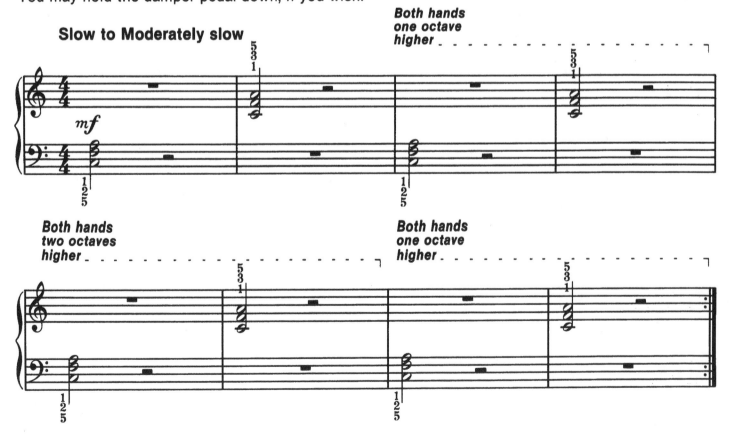

No. 3   Hands Together, Changing Octaves

Lift hands high.
You may hold the damper pedal down, if you wish.

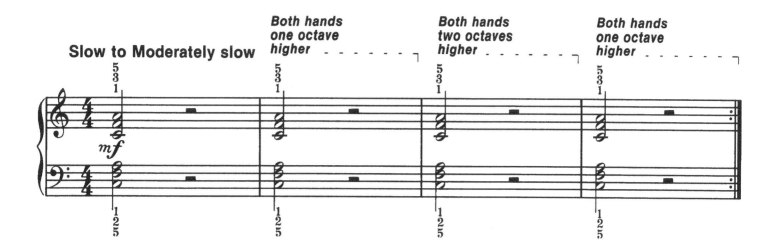

No. 4   Five-Finger Workout, Using the Notes of the C, F & G⁷ Chords

Play the first eight measures three times:

1. Soft, keeping fingers close to keys.
2. Moderately loud, lifting each finger about one inch above the key.
3. Loud, lifting each finger high.
   Play the final measure when you finish the third time.

Do NOT hold the damper pedal down in this exercise!

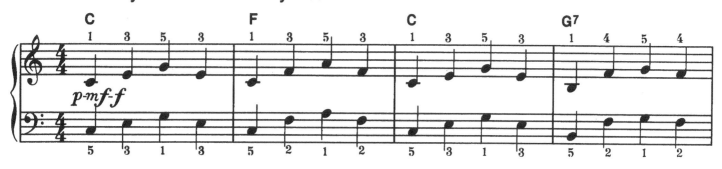

Use with pages 30 & 31.

Workouts in G Position

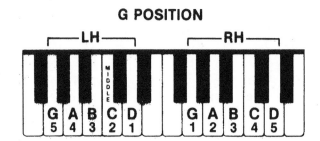

No. 1 Melodic & Harmonic Intervals

DROP into the thumb note, lift off after the second note, then drop into the harmonic intervals.
Play hands separately at first, then together.

No. 2 Harmonic Waltz

DROP into each harmonic interval. Connect the LH to the first RH interval in each measure.

*mf-p **means play** *moderately loud* **the first time, and** *soft* **the second time.**

No. 3 Five-Finger Workout in G Position

Play hands separately first, then together. The hands play identical fingerings at all times.

Moderately slow to Moderately fast

No. 4 Moving Up & Down in 3rds & 5ths

Keep the hand SHAPED as you DROP and LIFT on each interval. The hand position changes on each interval. You need only to read the notes played with the thumb and move the hand up or down.

Play hands separately, then together.

HARMONIC 3rds

Moderately slow to Moderately fast

HARMONIC 5ths

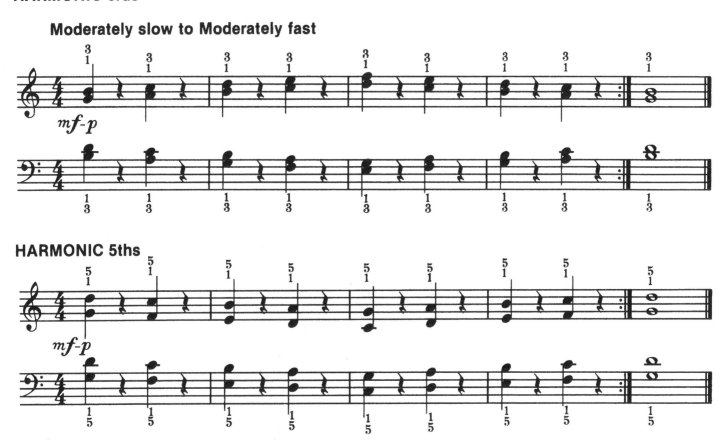

Use with pages 32 & 33.

The Problem of Developing Equal Skills with All Fingers

By this time you will realize that some fingers are more difficult to control than others.

The 5th finger is the smallest and weakest, and requires special exercise to develop strength equal to the others.

The 4th finger is the least independent finger, and the least agile. It is the only finger that is bound to its neighboring fingers by tendons that limit its movement.

The 3rd and 2nd fingers are the most agile fingers. They can move more easily through a larger arc. They are the strongest fingers.

The 1st finger (thumb) has its own problems. Its muscles are not designed to make it easy to strike a downward arc, but rather to pull the thumb inward, toward the palm. This makes it practical to turn the thumb under the fingers for playing scales, as you will see later, but in ordinary playing the thumb must strike on the side-tip, and is thus more awkward than the other fingers.

The following illustration shows the tendons of the left hand, as viewed from the back of the hand.

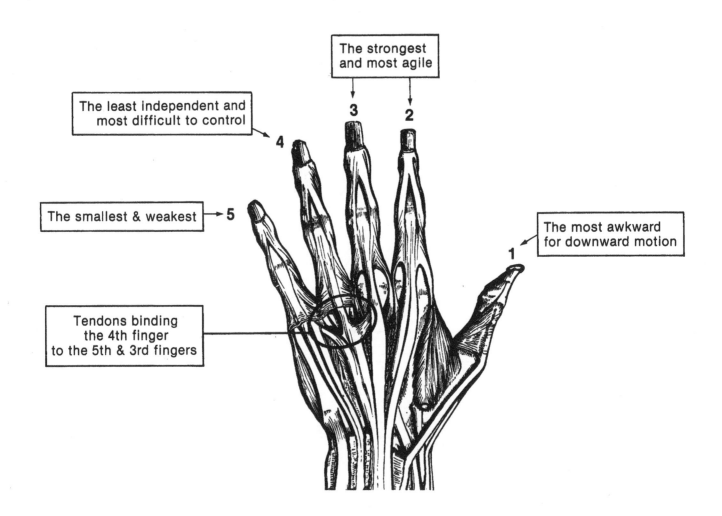

Illustration from "Gray's Anatomy"

NOTE: "Table-Top Aerobics," on page 48, will be beneficial in overcoming some of these problems.

A Leschetizky Solution

Theodor Leschetizky (1830–1915) was one of the most prestigious teachers of his time. Among his most famous pupils were Paderewski, Gabrilovich and Artur Schnabel. He was a genius at overcoming technical problems of each of his individual pupils, and one of his most effective exercises was specifically devised for developing skill and agility with all fingers and overcoming the problems of playing well with the weakest and most awkward fingers.

IMPORTANT! Read Leschetizky's own instructions carefully before playing:

While FOUR fingers hold the whole notes down, ONE finger plays the quarter notes.
Repeat each measure many times.

1. In the first measure, press down the five keys together (G F A B C, all the keys in G POSITION), then raise the thumb JUST HIGH ENOUGH TO LET THE KEY RISE TO ITS LEVEL, keeping the thumb in touch with it. Now the thumb presses the key down again, holds it a moment, then rises again.

2. Continue in the same manner with the 2nd finger, raising it about one-third of an inch and striking the key repeatedly while the other fingers hold their keys.

3. Proceed similarly with the 3rd finger, keeping the others down.

4. Now continue with the 4th finger, but raise it AS HIGH AS POSSIBLE, so that the hampered 4th finger may gain more independence.

5. Continue with the 5th finger, raising it also AS HIGH AS POSSIBLE, so that it may acquire more strength.

Keep fingers CURVED at all times.

Follow the same procedure as outlined above when playing with the left hand.

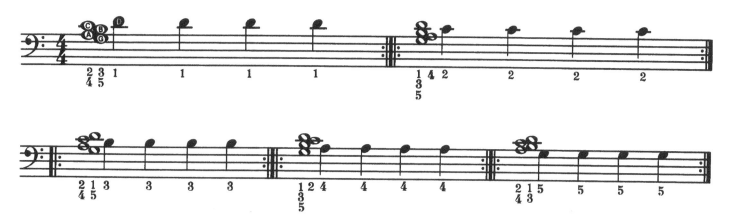

Use with pages 36 & 37.

Workouts With G Major & D⁷ Chords

No. 1   Building G Major & D⁷ Chords

LIFT after each three-note slur, then DROP into the chord.
Carefully observe *crescendos* and *diminuendos*.

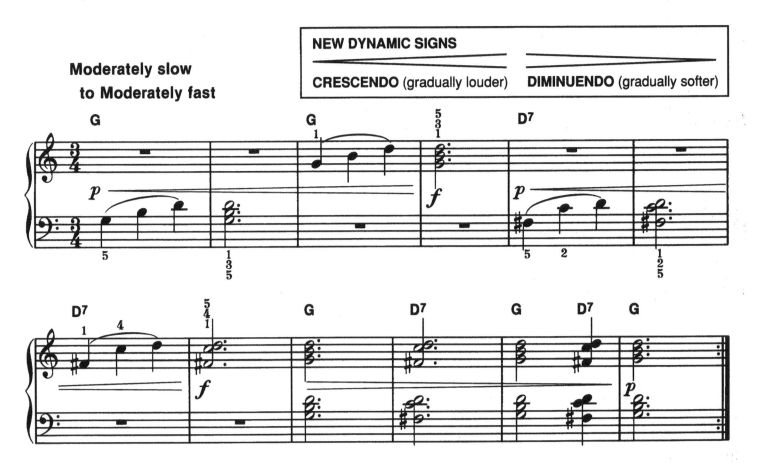

No. 2   RH Five-Finger Workout With LH Chords

Moderately slow to Moderately fast

No. 3 LH Five-Finger Workout with RH Chords

Moderately slow to Moderately fast

No. 4 Chord "Cross-Overs," with Pedal

Notice how much sound you can build with the pedal sustaining the chords.
In the 1st line, play each chord just a little louder than the one before.
In the 2nd line, play each chord a little softer.

Moderately slow

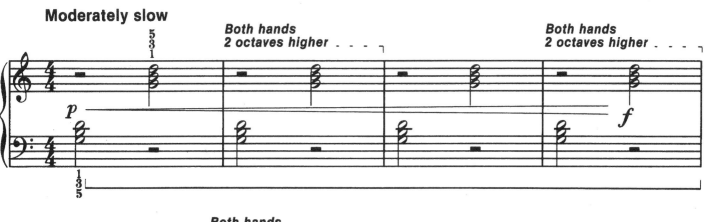

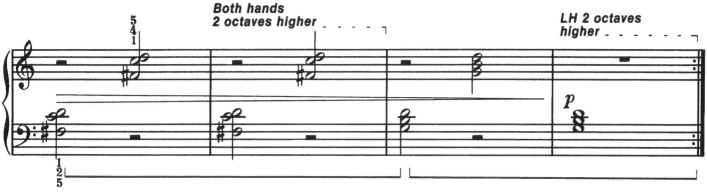

Use with pages 38 & 39.

Workouts with G Major, D⁷ & C Major Chords

No. 1   RH G, C & D⁷ Chords, Broken & Blocked

Moderately slow to Moderately fast

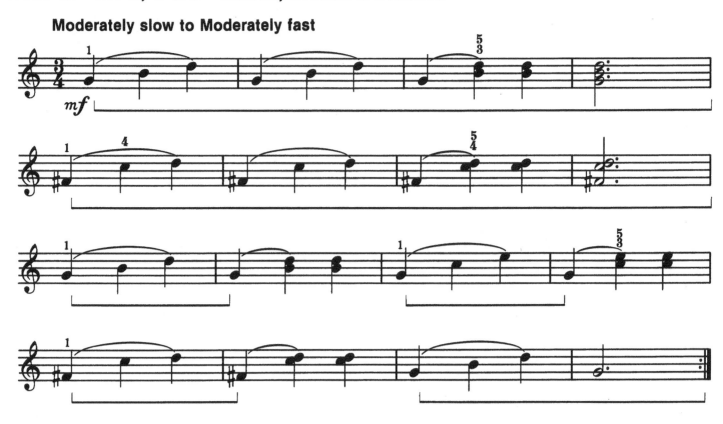

No. 2   LH G, C & D⁷ Chords, Broken & Blocked

Moderately slow to Moderately fast

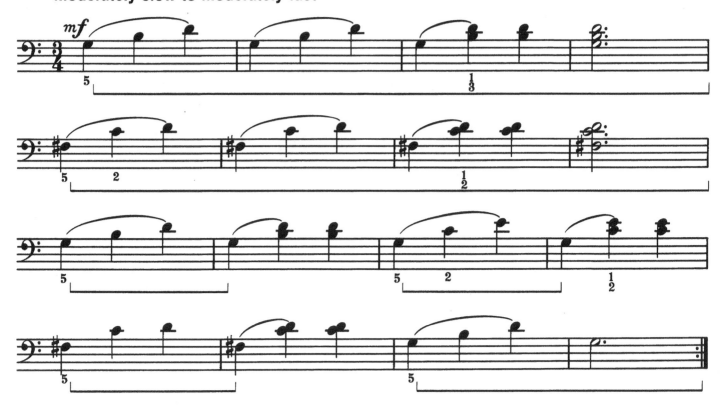

No. 3 "Aerobic Cross-Overs"

Moderately slow to Moderately fast

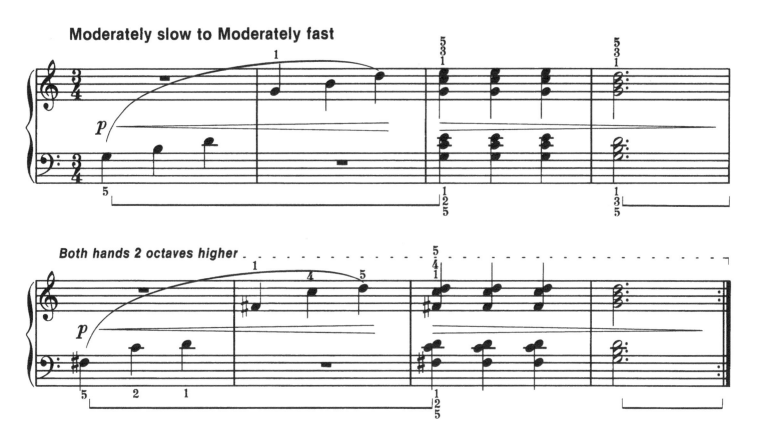

No. 4 Aerobic "On-Beat" & "After-Beat" Chords

Chords played on the 1st and 3rd beats are called "ON-BEAT" chords.
Chords played on the 2nd & 4th beats are called "AFTER-BEAT" chords.
LIFT & DROP on each chord.

Moderately slow to Moderately fast

BOTH HANDS 1 octave higher 2nd time

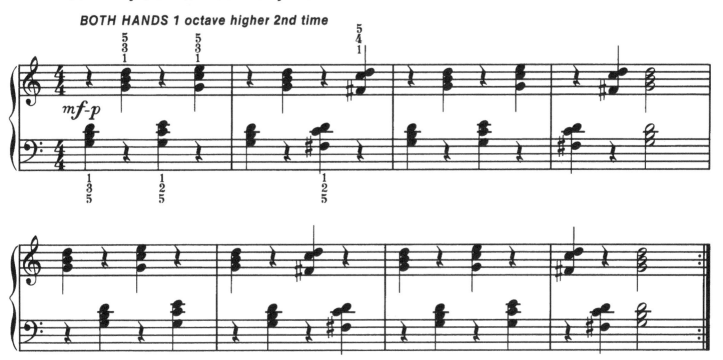

Middle C "Aerobics"

Use with pages 42–45.

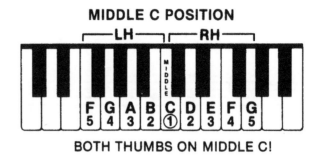

MIDDLE C POSITION

BOTH THUMBS ON MIDDLE C!

No. 1 Drops & Lifts

Hold the RH in position over the keys. DROP into first note. LIFT OFF the last note of the phrase, leading with a relaxed wrist. Let the fingers follow.

Repeat this procedure, beginning with the LH in position over the keys.

Moderately slow to Moderately fast

No. 2 Workout to Strengthen the 4th and 5th Fingers

Moderately slow to Moderately fast

No. 3   Theme in Middle C Position

DROP into the first note of each slurred group, and LIFT OFF the last, leading with a relaxed wirst.

Moderately to Moderately fast

No. 4   Variations on the Same Theme, with Eighth Notes   *(Add after page 45.)*

DROP into the first note of each slurred group, and LIFT OFF the last, leading with a relaxed wrist.

Moderately slow to Moderately fast

30

Use with page 46, and continue to use.

An Astonishing "Amadeus" Aerobic

Wolfgang Amadeus Mozart played with such astounding technical skill at the keyboard that his audiences were amazed.

Among Mozart's discoveries was an exercise that developed equal skill in all 10 fingers. Many famous keyboard artists had said that it was impossible to trill with the 4th and 5th fingers. Mozart could do this with ease, because he had found that by beginning with the stronger fingers and gradually substituting the neighboring finger, as shown in the exercise below, the skill of the more agile fingers could be "transferred" to the neighboring, weaker fingers.

Notice that the same two notes are used throughout the exercise, but the fingering changes on each line.

Begin slowly, so you can keep the same speed throughout. Keep the fingers very close to the keys, and play very legato. Keep the wrist very relaxed, and play the exercise with a smooth, even flow, without slowing down or stopping anywhere along the way.

No. 1   For Right Hand

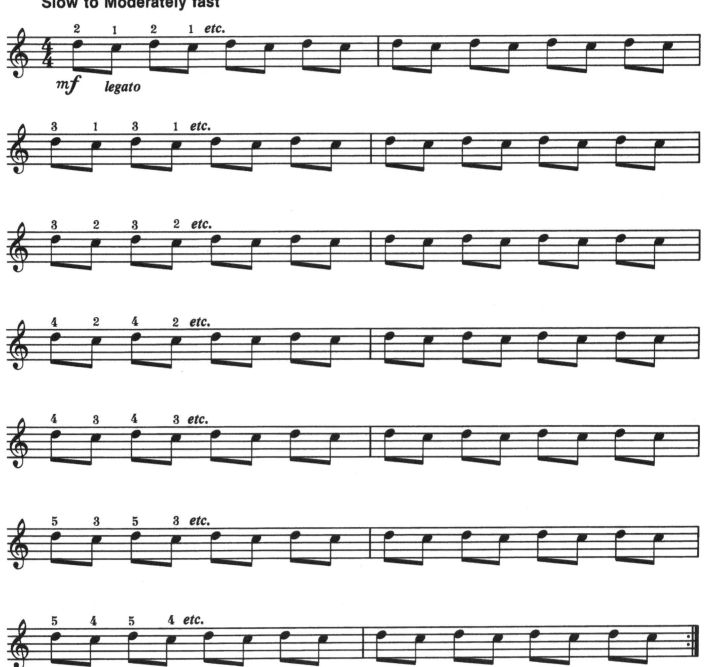

No. 2   For Left Hand

Slow to Moderately fast

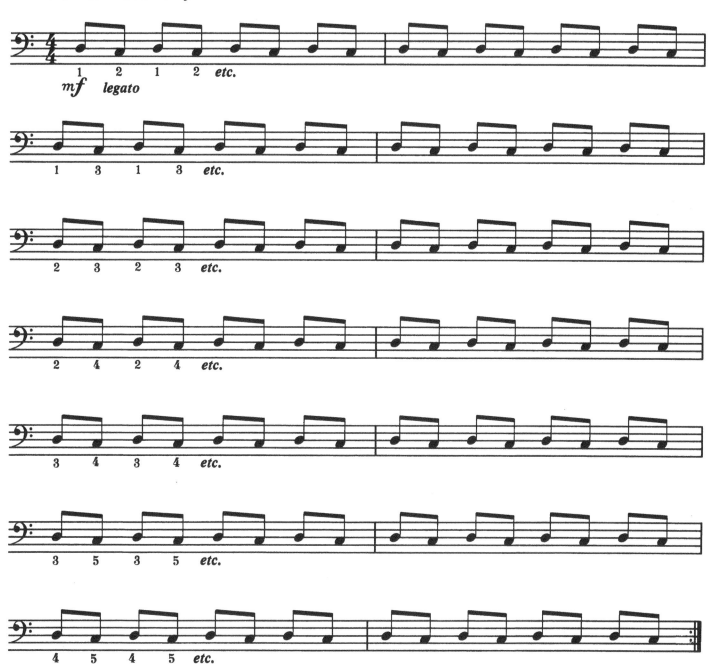

IMPORTANT!

After you can play these exercises smoothly with a moderately fast tempo, you may wish to use them to gain additional strength in the weaker fingers.

This can be accomplished by lifting the fingers higher.
Increase the volume bit by bit as you practice until you are playing *forte.*
Avoid doing this for long periods of time, however. Practicing any exercise too long may tire the hand and build tension in the fingers, wrists and arms, and this is detrimental to your progress.

From time to time it is advisable to stop and repeat the simple preliminary exercises on pages 2-4, "shaking out" the hands. This will relax the fingers, wrists and arms, and then you may find that you can continue without fatigue.

The Amazing Aerobics of Hanon

Use with page 47, and continue to use.

Charles-Louis Hanon, pronounced "ah-NON," (1819–1900), wrote, "The 4th and 5th fingers are almost useless because of the lack of special exercises to strenthen them." He then proceeded to devise some exercises that are so successful that they brought him worldwide fame. They are still used as warm-ups by the most skilled pianists of the present day.

No. 1

Skip the interval of a 3rd between LH 5 & 4 and between RH 1 & 2 on the first two notes of this exercise, then play up and down in 2nds. The LH 5 and RH 1 then fall on the note that was skipped in the first measure, and the hands move to a higher position in each following measure. After you reach the highest note of the exercise, descend by skipping a 3rd between RH 5 & 4, and between LH 1 & 2.

This remarkable exercise gives practice in stretching the LH 4th & 5th fingers while ascending and the 4th & 5th fingers of the RH while descending.

The exercise is so simple to grasp that you do not even have to look at the music to play it, and you can continue up the keyboard as far as you wish.

LIFT FINGERS HIGH and play each note distinctly. Practice slowly at first, then gradually increase speed.

Moderately slow to Moderately fast

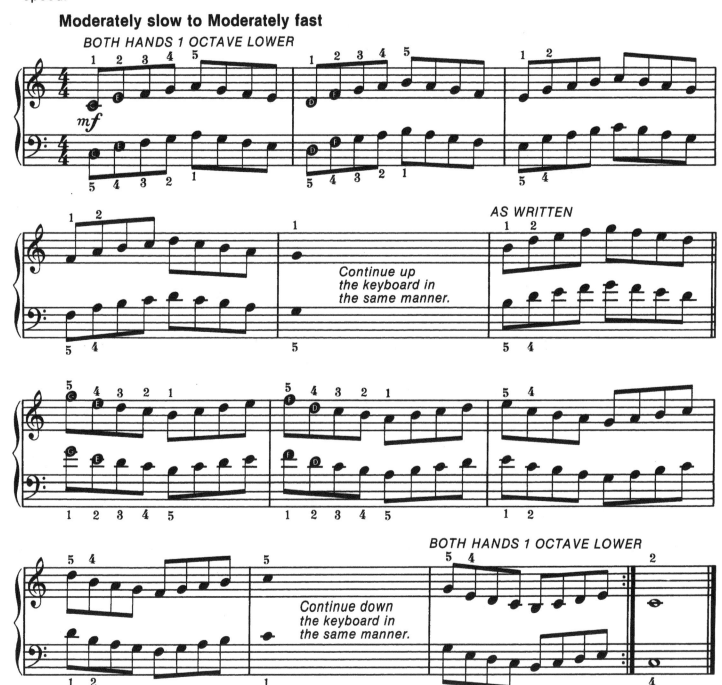

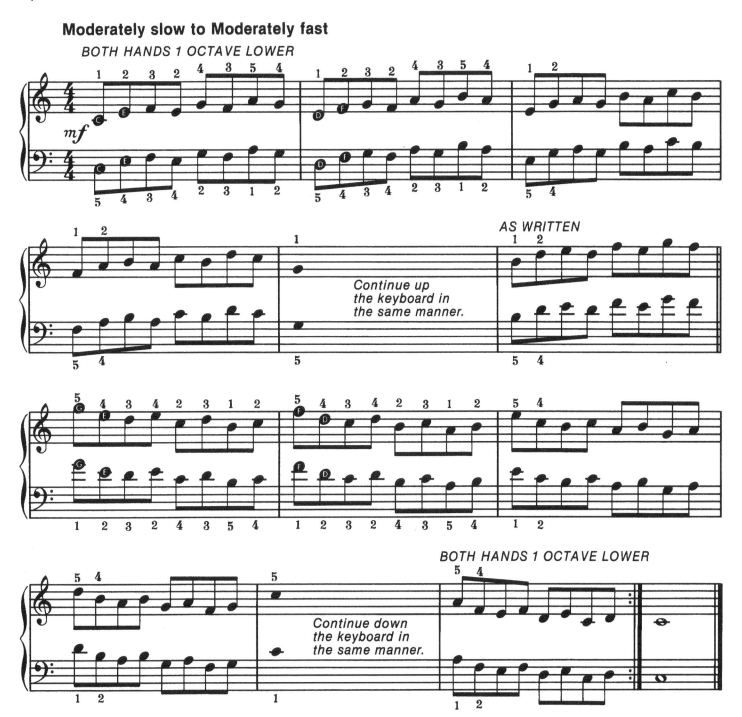

No. 2

This exercise is chosen from the HANON series because it uses the same system for moving up and down the keyboard as the previous one, and because it not only continues the stretch between the 5th and 4th fingers but also strengthens the remaining fingers equally.

Once you have grasped the pattern of the exercise you will not have to look at the music to play it. Continue up the keyboard as far as you wish.

LIFT FINGERS HIGH and play each note distinctly. Practice slowly at first, then gradually increase speed.

Moderately slow to Moderately fast

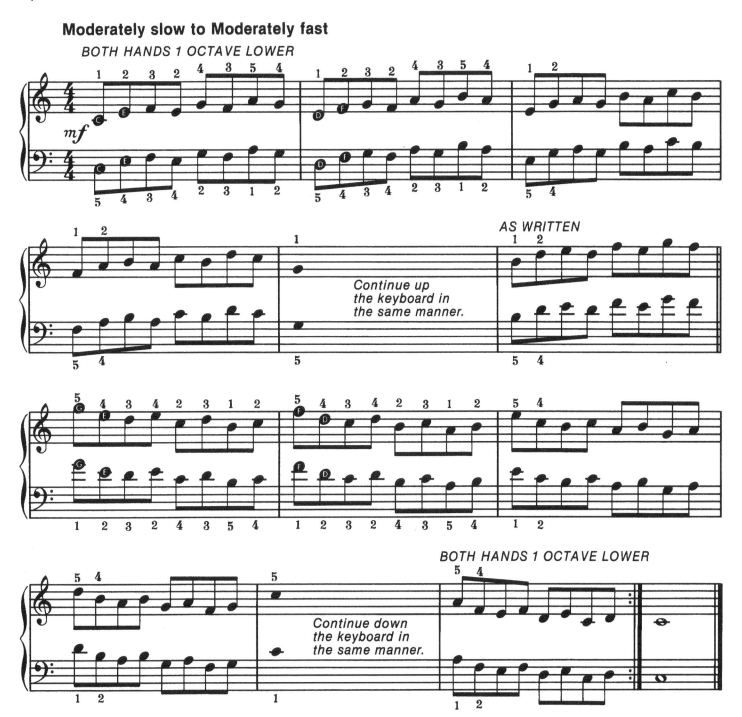

After you have learned to play Nos. 1 & 2 evenly, at a moderate speed, you may also benefit by practicing them softly, with the fingers close to the keys. Repeat very loud, lifting the fingers very high. It is also good to begin each exercise softly, making a gradual crescendo as you go higher, then gradually diminuendo as you come down again to the lowest notes. This builds great control of each finger muscle.

Dotted Aerobics

Use with pages 48–51.

No. 1 Dotted Rhythms in G Position & C Position

Position the hands over the keys before playing. LIFT on the half-rest, moving the hand over the keys of the new position.

Play the entire exercise twice (including the repeat):
1. Soft, with fingers close to the keys.
2. Loud and bold, lifting fingers high.

Moderately slow to Moderately fast

2nd TIME PLAY BOTH HANDS 1 OCTAVE LOWER

No. 2 Chords with Dotted Rhythms

Position the hands over each chord before playing. Repeat the chords by using flexible wrists. LIFT on the half-rests, moving over the next chord in advance.

The rhythm is the same as "Here Comes the Bride!" Play boldly, with confidence.

Moderately

2nd TIME PLAY BOTH HANDS 1 OCTAVE HIGHER

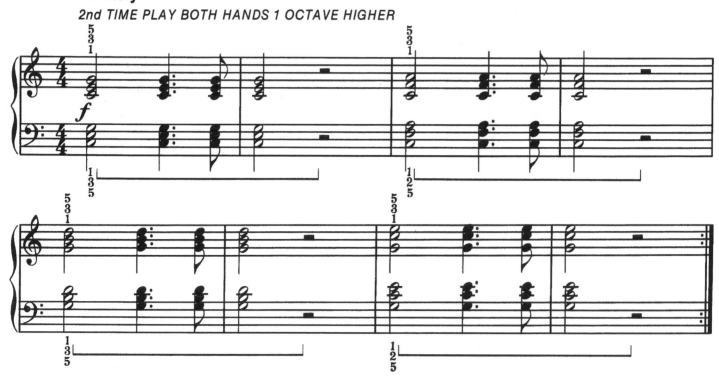

Use with page 52, and continue to use.

Hanon's Aerobic Sixths

This exercise will make you thoroughly familiar with the interval of a 6th, at the same time giving all fingers a great workout!

Notice how cleverly Hanon uses the 6th to raise the hands to the next higher position, then to lower them back again.

LIFT FINGERS HIGH. Play each note clearly and distinctly. Practice slowly, then gradually increase speed.

Moderately slow to Moderately fast

This exercise may be combined with Nos. 1 & 2 on pages 32 & 33, and it is excellent practice to play all three exercises continously, without stopping.

More exercises by Hanon may be found in Alfred publication No. 617, *Hanon, Book 1* or No. 616, *Hanon, THE VIRTUOSO PIANIST IN 60 EXERCISES (Complete Edition)*.

Use with pages 54–57.

Bartók's Wrist & Finger Aerobics

In 1913, the great Hungarian composer and pianist, Béla Bartók (1881–1945), wrote a book with Reschovsky, another Hungarian pianist, in which he gave specific instructions concerning those motions of the wrist and fingers he considered most fundamental to good piano performance. The following exercises are based on the principles he outlined.

No. 1 Notes Followed By Rests

The sign ⌒➘ indicates the raising and lowering of the wrist.
With the finger on the key and the wrist low, raise the wrist very gradually, allowing the finger to follow, then let it descend. (The finger touches the key *after* the wrist has begun its descent.)
Practice hands separately at first, then together.

Moderately slow

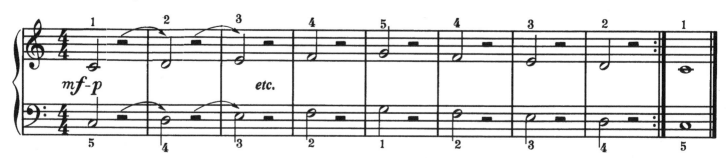

No. 2 Melodic Intervals Followed By Rests

The first note and each note following a rest should be played from the wrist. The fingers of both hands must play at exactly the same moment. No deviation, however small, must be allowed between the action of the two hands.

Moderately slow

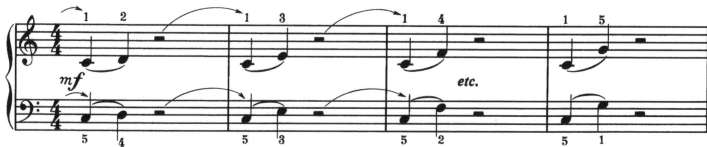

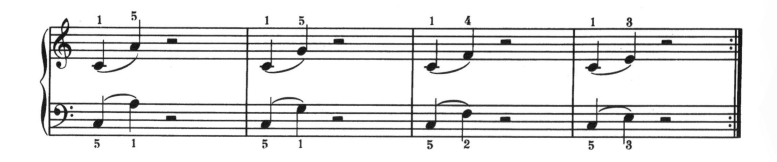

No. 3 Finger-Staccato *(Add with page 57.)*

When staccato notes occur without rest between them, move only the fingers to play the staccato. After touching each key, the finger returns to a raised position. The wrist remains quiet. All movements should be completely relaxed, without stiffness or forcing.

Practice hands separately at first, then together.

Moderately slow to Moderately fast

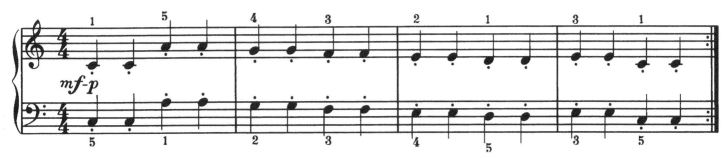

No. 4 Wrist-Staccato

When a rest occurs after a staccato note, the hand should rebound with a relaxed wrist motion, as if it were thrown into its raised position immediately after touching the key, like a rubber ball rebounding.

Practice hands separately at first, then together.

a) Single notes.

Moderately slow to Moderately fast

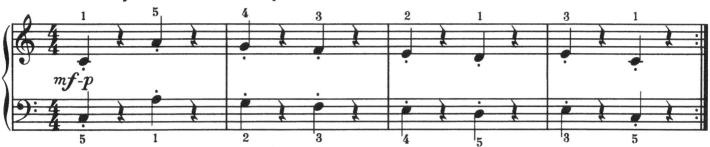

b) Melodic 6ths.

Moderately slow to Moderately fast

Additional Bartók exercises may be found in Alfred publication No. 1730, *Bartók, AN INTRODUCTION TO HIS PIANO WORKS.*

Use with pages 58 & 59.

Stretching Exercises: 2nds to Octaves

Play these exercises using the principles outlined by Bartók. (See pages 36 & 37).
Practice hands separately at first, then together.

No. 1   Melodic Intervals

Moderately slow to Moderately fast

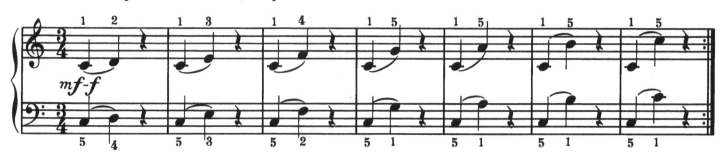

No. 2   Harmonic Intervals

Moderately slow to Moderately fast

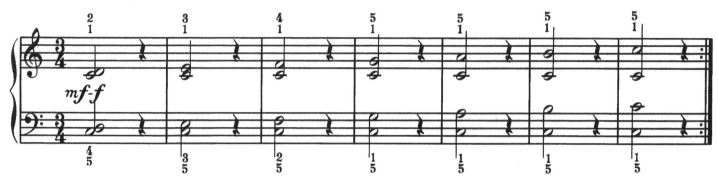

No. 3   Staccato Notes (Finger-staccato)

Moderately slow to Moderately fast

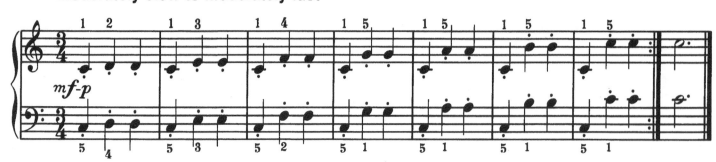

These Hands Were Made for Playing

The fact that the thumb opposes the remaining fingers is one of the significant differences between humans and animals. It enables us to use tools skillfully, to write and paint, and also to make music. It is a particularly important factor in playing a keyboard instrument.

The musculature of the hand allows the thumb to pivot under the palm of the hand and easily touch the base of the 4th finger. By making use of this facility, we have the ability to turn the thumb to play a key, and then we can shift the position of the hand. This enables us to play continuously up or down the entire piano keyboard.

The following drawings are views of the PALM of the hand.

The drawing on the left shows the *palmar fascia,* the connective tissue that supports the muscles of the inner part of the hand.

The drawing on the right shows how the thumb reaches under to the base of the 4th finger to play scales of eight or more notes without interrupting the flow of the notes.

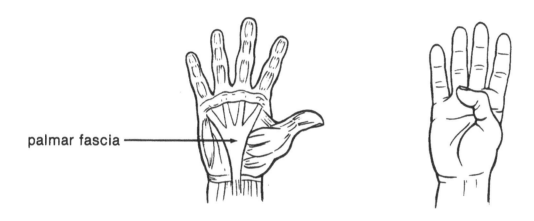

palmar fascia

The C Major Scale

As soon as the thumb has played the first note (while the 2nd finger is playing the second note), pivot the thumb under to the base of the 4th finger, so it will be ready to play its next note in advance.

This is one of the most important secrets of smooth, legato scale playing!

Moderately slow

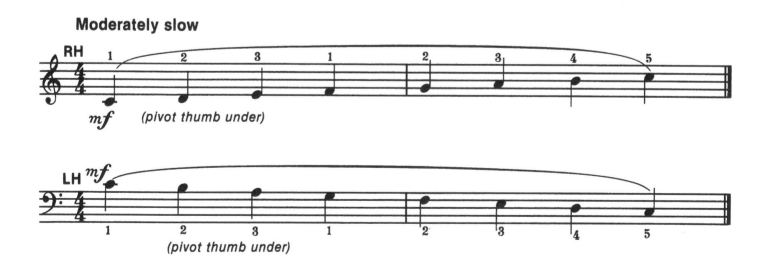

(pivot thumb under)

(pivot thumb under)

Scale Aerobics

These four exercises will make scale playing easy. Practice them daily, for several weeks.

It is important to occasionally review the PRELIMINARY EXERCISES on pages 2 & 3, especially before and after practicing these "scale aerobics."

No. 1   Thumb-Unders

Start the thumb-under motion just as you play the harmonic 2nd on the 2nd beat of each measure. The thumb should be over the key played on the 3rd beat well in advance. Keep the wrist loose and quiet. LIFT OFF on the 4th count.

Moderately slow to Moderately fast

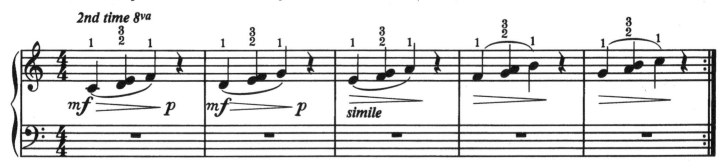

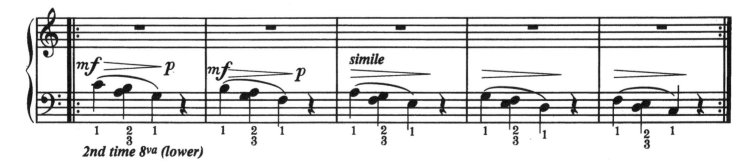

No. 2   Scale Improver

This is certain to make scales much easier. On the last count of the 3rd measure of each line, shift the hand in one smooth and secure motion to play the 2nd and 5th fingers together.

Moderately slow to Moderately fast

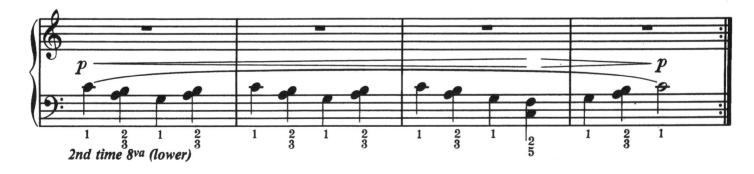

No. 3   Get Ready — Go!

Notice how easily you play the scale after playing the first two measures of each line!
Lean the hand slightly in the direction you are moving. Avoid any twisting motion of the wrists.

Moderately slow to Moderately fast

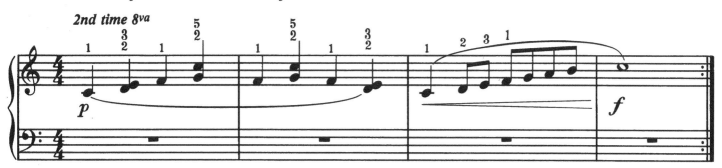

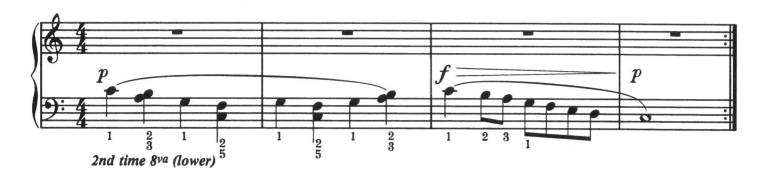

No. 4   Technic Builder

RH & LH play same fingers at the same time throughout. Play hands separately at first.

When you play hands together a while, try for SPEED, but play only as fast as you can play with the hands EXACTLY TOGETHER.

Moderately slow to Fast

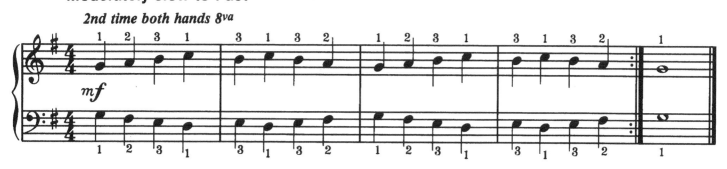

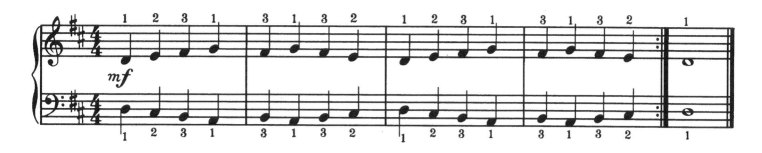

Broken Triad Aerobics

Use with pages 64 & 65.

No. 1   Broken Triads, Moving Up the Keyboard

The hand position changes in each measure.

While holding each half note, shift RH 1 and LH 5 one white key higher, to be ready for the first note of the next measure.

While playing the first quarter note of the next measure, move the remaining fingers over the keys that complete the chord.

Press into the keys to get the "feel" of each triad.

Moderately slow to Moderately fast

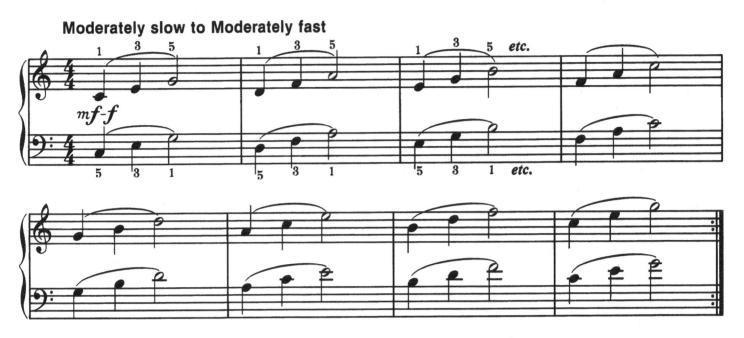

No. 2   Broken Triads, Hand to Hand

As the RH plays the 2nd measure, move the LH fingers one white key higher, over the notes of the 3rd measure. As the LH plays the 3rd measure, move the RH in position for the next measure, etc.

Always remember to breath normally. Try inhaling on the first two measures and exhaling on the next two. Discover the breathing that is right for YOU.

When this exercise is played properly, the notes seem to FLOW up the keyboard!

Moderately slow to Moderately fast

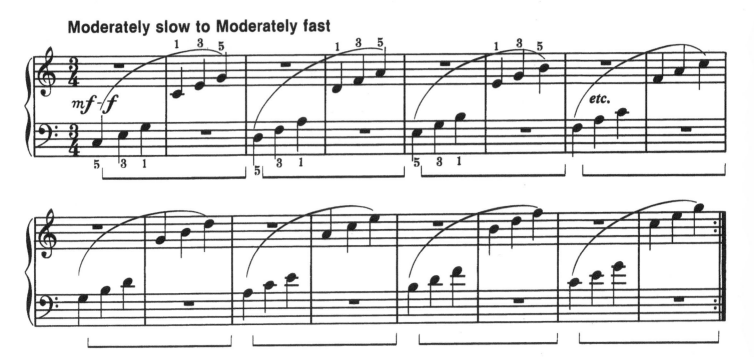

"Alberti Aerobics"

"Alberti bass" is a name given to a LH accompaniment figure in which the notes of a broken chord are played in this order: lowest, highest, middle, highest. It is named for Domenico Alberti (1710–1740), an Italian composer who was the first to make frequent use of it. It is found in the music of Haydn, Mozart, Clementi, and many other classical composers of the late 18th and early 19th century.

No. 1 Meet Alberti

Practice the LH alone at first, very legato, with an even, relaxed touch, then add the RH. The notes of the two hands must sound exactly together.

Moderately slow to Moderately

No. 2 "Alberti Blues" *(Add with page 67.)*

Alberti bass, usually found in classical sonatas and sonatinas, also works well with the BLUES.

Try practicing this two ways: **a)** with even notes, and **b)** with the eighth notes played a bit unevenly; *long   short long   short, etc.*

Slow blues tempo

44

Extended Positions

Use with pages 68 & 69, and continue to practice.

When the hand plays a four note chord made up of the ROOT, 3rd, 5th & OCTAVE, an EXTENDED POSITION must be used.

No. 1   Extended Positions with All White Keys

When the chord uses white keys only, the RH fingering is 1 2 3 5.
The LH fingering is 5 4 2 1.

Practice hands separately at first, positioning the fingers over the four notes of the chord before playing, if possible. Then practice hands together.

Slow to Moderately fast

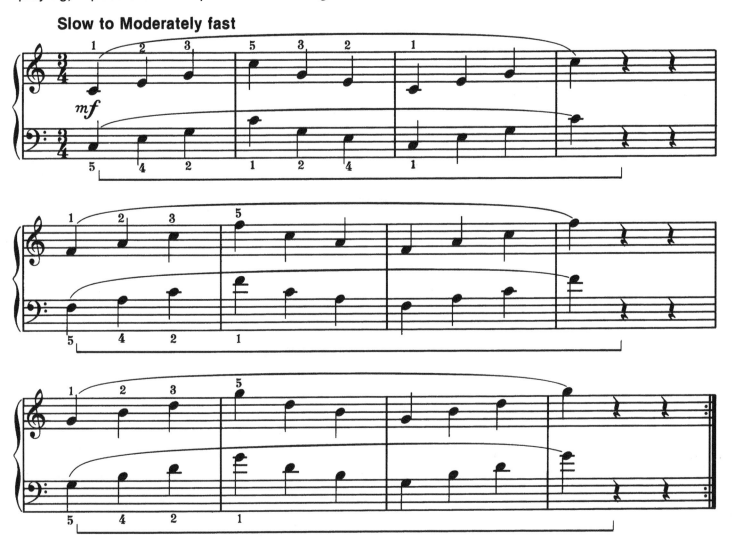

No. 2   Extended Position with Black Key 3rd

When the 3rd of the chord is a BLACK KEY, the RH fingering is still 1 2 3 5.
The LH fingering is 5 3 2 1.

Practice hands separately at first, then together.

Slow to Moderately fast

Use with pages 71 & 72, and continue to practice.

Changing Fingers On Repeated Notes

Often it is convenient to change fingers on repeated notes. This is important because repeating notes rapidly with the same finger can produce tension in the wrists as well as the fingers.

The following exercise also helps to strengthen the 4th finger and to make its agility match that of the 3rd and 2nd fingers. Use this exercise to prepare for the LISZT "Aerobics" below.

Begin very slowly. Gradually increase speed.

Liszt's "Aerobics" for Repeated Notes

Franz Liszt (1811–1886) probably had more agile fingers than any other pianist. For many years he applied himself to divising and practicing exercises. The following are derived from many he developed for playing rapidly repeated notes.

Liszt left the following instructions:

These exercises should be played in two ways:
   a) with a quiet wrist and high finger action.
   b) with the wrist moving in a single upward and downward motion, with fingers curling inward toward the hand. (This should resemble "wiping the surface of the key.")

No. 1   Repeating with 4 3 2 1

Practice hands separately at first, then precisely together.

Slow to as Fast as possible

No. 2   Repeating with 5 4 3 2

Practice hands separately, then together.

Slow to as Fast as possible

Additional Liszt exercises may be found in Alfred publication No. 630, *Liszt, TECHNICAL EXERCISES (COMPLETE),* and No. 583, *Liszt, TECHNICAL EXERCISES (ABRIDGED).* These are quite difficult, but you may wish to try them when you become more advanced.

Use with page 75, and continue to practice.

Daily Scale Practice

Daily workouts with scales played in various rhythms are very beneficial, and will help you with ALL the music you play.

Placing accents on different notes will help you develop equal strength in all fingers, and when you play scales in even, unaccented rhythms, you will see that you have improved.

3rd fingers are circled in these scales to show that the 3rd fingers of the RH and LH always play together in these scales.

To get the maximum benefit from these scales, practice them legato: **a)** with the fingers close to the keys, and **b)** with fingers lifted high.

If you were Franz Liszt, you would probably also practice them staccato.

No. 1   Scale with Dotted Rhythms and Accents

Practice hands separately, then together.

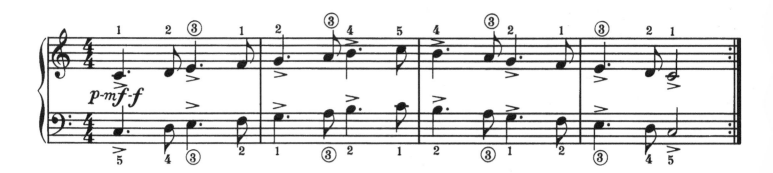

No. 2   Scale with Shifted Dotted Rhythms and Accents

Practice hands separately, then together.

No. 3 Scale with Quarter and Eighth Note Rhythms

Notice how the accents fall in different places as you move up and down the scale.

Practice hands separately, then together.

No. 4 Scale with Triplets *(Add with page 94.)*

This is a bit tricky to play with hands together, so prepare well by practicing hands separately many times.

You may apply these same exercises to all the major and minor scales shown on page 96 of Adult Lesson Book 1. By studying this page you will see that the 3rd fingers of the RH and LH occur together in all the scales shown except the F Major Scale.

48

Table-Top Aerobics

These are exercises you can do AWAY FROM THE PIANO. Begin them ANYTIME!

Play each exercise as follows:

Place the hand lightly on a table top, book, or other flat surface.
Imagine you are in C POSITION, with the fingers on neighboring keys: C D E F G.
Let the wrist also rest on the surface.
Play each exercise, tapping each finger *lightly.* Avoid pressing into the surface.

No. 1 Keep the THUMB on the table as you tap the fingers indicated.

No. 2 Keep the 5th finger on the table.

No. 3 Keep 1, 2 & 5 on the table.

No. 4 Keep 1, 2 & 3 on the table. (Tricky, but it will strengthen 4 & 5.)